Scaling Agile: A Lean JumpStart

Sanjiv Augustine

Scaling Agile: A Lean JumpStart

Sanjiv Augustine

This book is for sale at
http://leanpub.com/ScalingAgileALeanJumpStart

This version was published on 2015-09-30

ISBN 978-1-329-40550-9

Leanpub

This is a Leanpub book. Leanpub empowers authors and
publishers with the Lean Publishing process. Lean Publishing is
the act of publishing an in-progress ebook using lightweight tools
and many iterations to get reader feedback, pivot until you have
the right book and build traction once you do.

for my father Dr. John Sunderaj Augustine

Contents

1. Introduction   3

2. Can We Scale Agile Methods Up from Teams?   5

3. Scaling Agile Requires Changing the System   9

4. Scaling Agile - Starting Lean   15
   4.1. Limit WIP   20
   4.2. Manage the Flow   24
   4.3. Grow Small, Stable Teams   28
   4.4. Build a Network of Small Teams   31
   4.5. Improve Continuously   35

5. Overview of Scaling Techniques and Frameworks . . .   39
   5.1. The Scrum of Scrums Meeting   41
   5.2. The Lean-Agile Program Management Office (PMO)   42
   5.3. The Spotify Model   44
   5.4. The Scaled Agile Framework® (SAFe®)   46
   5.5 Large Scale Scrum (LeSS)   48
   5.6. Disciplined Agile Delivery (DAD)   50
   5.7. Scaled Professional Scrum - Nexus™   51

References   53

About   55

About TechWell   57

Foreword

Now that agile practices are clearly in the mainstream, many organizations are attempting to apply agile on large projects and in groups of related projects. Although there are anecdotal examples of success scaling agile, many organizations are struggling, having only limited success, or even regressing to old waterfall methods. In *Scaling Agile: A Lean Jumpstart,* Sanjiv Augustine delivers practical advice on using lean development principles to enable the organizational culture changes often necessary for success.

The biggest challenge for executive management is to recognize that agile approaches such as Scrum and Kanban are necessary—but not sufficient—practices for implementing large scale agile adoption. Surveys about agile adoption show that management support and technical issues are often not the problem. Rather, it's the inability to change organizational culture and long-held beliefs that can cripple or kill an agile adoption program. Organizations that have adopted an agile mindset from top to bottom succeed. But how?

Based on his experiences with agile adoption successes and failures in multiple large organizations, Sanjiv Augustine believes that the most assured path to scaled agile is to use the Lean Thinking practices to drive the necessary cultural changes within the organization. This approach is not a cookie-cutter methodology. Instead, it's a concerted effort to lay the groundwork for agile and and adopt a continuous improvement path within and across the organization.

If you're wondering whether or not your organization is already aligned for scaled agile adoption, I suggest you turn to page eight and take the short survey on Symptoms of Organizational Misalignment. Then, on page thirteen read a short summary of what Lean Thinking is all about before diving into the five critical lean practices that can start you on the right path or provide a midcourse correction.

The last section of *Scaling Agile: A Lean Jumpstart* offers a quick overview of seven popular agile scaling technologies and frameworks. Although any of these methods may work in a given situation, Sanjiv rightly states that the best method is the one that is most easily customizable to your organization so you can continuously improve through incremental adaptation. In other words, one size definitely does not fit all.

Wayne Middleton

CEO, TechWell Corporation and Software Quality Engineering

September 2015

1. Introduction

Scrum, XP, and Kanban are now familiar Agile methods. In recent years, many have begun scaling their early agile adoptions beyond individual teams to programs, portfolios, and the enterprise. Agile must be paralleled by a simultaneous change in organizational culture, which can begin at the team level. So, even lacking initial top-down support, empowered small teams can begin an Agile transformation.

However, to truly scale Agile methods up, systemic changes are needed beyond Agile teams and across the organization. To drive these changes, several scaling techniques and frameworks exist, including the Scaled Agile Framework (SAFe), Large-Scale Scrum (LeSS), Disciplined Agile Delivery (DAD); as well as the simple Scrum of Scrums (SoS) meeting.

In this *JumpStart,* we'll explore how to lay a set of "building blocks" as an essential foundation for larger frameworks. These building block practices are:

1. Limit Work in Process (WIP);
2. Manage the Flow;
3. Grow Small, Stable Teams;
4. Build a Network of Teams; and
5. Improve Continuously.

By **building essential discipline around this set of key practices,** we can greatly enhance the chances of successfully scaling our Agile adoptions. Once these practices are in place, scaling using one of the frameworks becomes much simpler, and represents an easier organizational transition.

2. Can We Scale Agile Methods Up from Teams?

Some organizations have successfully scaled Agile up across projects, programs and to the enterprise, but many others struggle to make the organizational transition.

Created in 2001, the *Manifesto for Agile Software Development*[1] resonated with a generation of engineers who wanted to deliver customer value, and was stymied in that quest by the heavyweight methods of the time. Based on the Manifesto, Agile methods including Scrum, eXtreme Programming, Kanban, Crystal, DSDM, and Feature-Driven Development (See *Figure 1. Agile Methodology Used for Relative Adoption*) promoted adaptive planning, evolutionary development and delivery, a time-boxed iterative approach, and encouraged rapid and flexible response to change.

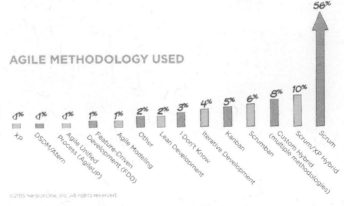

Figure 1. Agile Methodology Used, VersionOne Survey 2014

Industry leaders like Sales Force, Yahoo, Google, Capital One and

---

[1] http://www.agilemanifesto.org/

others discovered that, when implemented appropriately, Agile methods accelerate project delivery times, increase customer and employee satisfaction, and enable flexible changes in business requirements. These companies adopted Agile methods and, as a result, realized faster throughput and higher business customer satisfaction on individual projects. Based on this momentum, the move toward Agile methods is now a widespread industry phenomenon.

How about scaling Agile methods up from use on one team to multiple projects and multiple teams? It turns out that **large-scale adoptions of Agile methods are growing steadily in number**, as in *Figure 2. Agile on Multiple Projects and Teams.* Consider for instance that Nationwide Insurance has over 130 teams using Agile methods, and that Sales Force has over 200 teams that have implemented Agile.

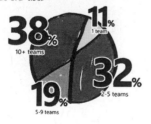

Figure 2. Agile on Multiple Projects and Teams

So clearly, sustained large-scale initiatives to adopt and successfully scale Agile methods are growing in number. That's the good news.

The bad news is that despite this significant success over nearly two decades, there are barriers to further adoption, as seen in *Figure*

3. Barriers to Agile Adoption, VersionOne Survey. Note that the **inability to change organizational culture** is identified as the leading barrier to further agile adoption.

BARRIERS TO FURTHER AGILE ADOPTION?

Figure 3. Barriers to Agile Adoption, VersionOne Survey 2014

Interestingly, VersionOne's past surveys reveal that organizational culture has been the leading barrier to further adoption of Agile methods since the inception of the survey several years ago. That is, a **mismatch with organizational culture has been the leading obstacle to successful Agile adoption for several years now.** Now, how is it that some companies are able to scale Agile up while others struggle?

Here's the answer – organizations that scale Agile successfully **have been using elements of Lean Thinking to make systemic changes, and thereby overcome cultural barriers.** That is, scaling Agile up requires **changing the traditional management system** set in place to govern traditional waterfall development.

Let's explore this concept further in the next section.

3. Scaling Agile Requires Changing the System

Scaling Agile requires changes in mindset and organizational culture that have to be driven by systemic changes to organizational structure and processes.

In my teens, I was a pretty good badminton player. My friends and I would meet every evening and we would play badminton for hours on end, and then hang out together. It was a fun and memorable time. Then a couple of us moved on, and I tried to take up tennis. I expected to learn tennis fairly quickly, but found myself struggling. Unfortunately, the wrist movements that made me a good badminton player limited my skill at tennis. It took me quite a while to realize that there was a mismatch between my badminton skills, and the different tools and techniques needed for tennis (See *Figure 4*). These two sports, while similar on the surface, have totally different movements, different gear (balls versus shuttlecocks, differently shaped and weighted racquets), and differently sized courts. Moving from badminton to tennis is therefore **not a trivial transition, and requires understanding these differences and making mental and structural changes to accommodate them.**

Figure 4. Badminton and Tennis Require Different Tools and Techniques

Clearly, not making these changes will impede an effective transition from one sport to the other, no matter how good the player. Seems obvious, right? Well, consider that a similar mismatch is playing out today in many organizations. **Traditional management techniques are being applied agile teams with adverse results, and perhaps inadvertently, crushing organizational agility.**

Here's what it looked like Acme Corporation, a fictitious company, based on several real-life experiences.

Several years ago, some developers at Acme Corporation experimented with eXtreme Programming (XP). They were interested in developing high quality code, and adopted XP without wider support. Without wider understanding and support, the XP adoption lost steam and pretty much petered out. Some of the XP developers became dispirited and left the organization. Others went underground and were practicing XP in solitude. The only thing people remembered about XP, is that "they used to practice pair programming."

Then, a few years ago, a motivated manager at Acme got wind of Scrum, the leading Agile method, and took a Certified ScrumMaster (CSM) class. She returned fired up, and implemented Scrum on her team. The team's morale went way up and they started to increase momentum with their project and product delivery. Their business customers were happy, and went around testifying to the benefits of Scrum and Agile methods.

From there, Scrum adoption spread virally from team to team, until a department head noticed that Scrum teams were delivering better results than their peers using traditional Waterfall, and their business customers were happier to boot. He connected with the Agile teams, and took on the mantle of Agile Champion. Under his leadership, several more teams adopted Scrum, and many integrated XP practices like *refactoring, test-driven development and continuous integration.* The XP developers were emboldened enough to come out of hiding, and now practiced their art in public. Product quality spiked, and business customers reported quicker delivery and better quality due to automated build-and-test cycles. This continued for over a year, and the department became noted for its agility and responsive to changing business and organizational needs.

Then inevitably, since this was a bottom-up adoption of Agile methods, problems arose as traditional management was over-laid on the agile teams.

It started with a reorganization that moved the Agile champion to another division. The new department head, while wanting to support Agile, didn't have a full understanding of Agile methods, and their underlying Lean principles. Without management that understood Agile and Lean, Agile practices began to erode, and fundamental organizational changes evolved as a traditional organizational structure grew on top of the agile teams. So, now Agile teams faced issues caused by misalignment with Agile tenets as listed in *Figure 5. Symptoms of Organizational Misalignment with Agile Methods.*

Symptoms of Organizational Misalignment with Agile Methods

1. While Agile methods call for small teams (5-9 people, for Scrum) average team size has grown to 25 people.

2. While Agile methods call for integrated teams with all necessary disciplines represented on the core team, testers have been pulled out of the formerly fully integrated team core, and are now in a separate Quality Assurance (QA) silo.

3. While Agile methods call for team allocation of 80% or more for the core team to a single effort, team members are now multitasking on 2-3 projects at a time.

4. While Agile methods call for locking down scope within a Sprint or Iteration, untrained product owners introduce new user stories while Sprints or Iterations are underway.

5. While Agile methods call for "accepted responsibility" and indicate that team members should handle work assignments amongst themselves, newly hired **project managers** are assigning work top-down to team members in Sprint/Iteration planning meetings.

6. While Agile methods call for Daily Standup meetings to be run by the team, they have devolved into status meetings for the project managers.

Figure 5. Symptoms of Organizational Misalignment with Agile Methods.

Do you recognize these symptoms? Sadly, they're pretty typical for an organization that has **failed to prepare its middle and** upper management for agile methods. So, unprepared managers drive agile methods using traditional techniques, introduce traditional structures on top of the Agile teams, and cause the organization to regress in its Agile adoption.

We end up with an organization that looks like the one in *Figure 6. Traditional Waterfall Management Overlaid on Agile Teams.*

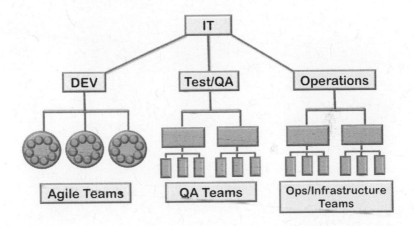

Figure 6. Traditional Waterfall Management Overlaid on Agile Teams

Unfortunately, this overlay introduces a self-reinforcing loop between culture and organizational structure. Since organizational structure drives culture, **the traditional structure eventually drives Agile teams back to Waterfall.**

To arrest this backsliding to Waterfall, we have to **reinforce and amplify Agile beyond the team**, as covered next.

4. Scaling Agile - Starting Lean

Scaling Agile requires extending and amplifying Agile Methods beyond the Team at the program and portfolio levels.

Modern Agile methods, including Scrum and XP, all have common elements in the 'Evo' (short form for **Evo**lutionary Value Delivery) methodology, created by Tom Gilb in 1960. Two pivotal concepts in Evo are:

· **Incremental product delivery**: delivering products to market in small chunks called iterations; and

· **Process iteration**: going through the entire software lifecycle of planning, design, development, test and ready at a micro level, repeatedly, in a short timebox.

Evo, in turn, drew its inspiration from the work of W. Edwards Deming with Total Quality Management (TQM). At the heart of Deming's work is the Plan-Do-Check-Act (PDCA) improvement loop, illustrated in *Figure 7. Deming's PDCA Improvement Loop.*

Deming Cycle

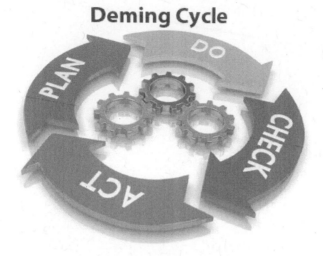

Figure 7. Deming's PDCA Improvement Loop

As we begin to scale Agile methods up from the team level, our goal is to **scale process iteration and incremental product delivery through the consolidated efforts of multiple teams in the best way possible.**

At a minimum this means **we need to institute a basic process framework across multiple teams and iterate upon it to continuously improve it.** This scaled framework needs to:

· Aggregate the work of multiple teams in the most productive way possible;

· Help us evolve the best suited organizational structure beyond the team;

· Ensure that the energy and passion on our Agile teams is amplified and not dampened; and

· Provide the best way for management to drive significant value.

At Toyota in post-World War II Japan, Deming also worked with Taichi Ohno and Shigeo Shingo; and together they created the famous Toyota Production System (TPS), known to the West as Lean Thinking. Key concepts of Lean Thinking are captured in *Figure 8. Lean Thinking.*

What is Lean Thinking?

Lean Thinking is the term popularized decades ago by Jim Womack and Dan Jones in their book of the same name (Simon & Schuster, 1996) for the **Toyota Production System (TPS)**, now known as the **Toyota Way**.

Lean Thinking has two pillars: **respect for people** and **continuous improvement**; and five core principles:

> 1. Specify **value** by product. Customer value is paramount, and provides the primary perspective of lens from which we view our process and delivery.
>
> 2. Identify the **value stream** for each product. We seek to identify the complete of steps to deliver customer value from idea inception to product delivery.
>
> 3. Make value **flow** without interruptions. We improve our process by identifying; and reducing or eliminating bottlenecks that impede the flow of value.
>
> 4. Let the customer **pull** value from the producer. We further reduce waste and improve productivity by carrying the least amount of inventory, and optimizing the way we work as a team to process it.
>
> 5. **Pursue perfection.** Teams and management pursue improvement relentlessly and continuously.

TPS and its supporting Lean culture, first set in place at Toyota after World War II, continues to drive Toyota's incredible success even today.

Figure 8. Lean Thinking

We can apply Lean Thinking to give us a set of minimal practices as we seek to create a basic framework and jumpstart a scaling effort. Specifically, we can apply Lean Thinking principles and generate this set of critical practices:

1. Limit Work in Process (WIP);
2. Manage the Flow;
3. Grow Small, Stable Teams;
4. Build a Network of Teams; and
5. Improve Continuously.

Next, we'll explore each of the above critical practices in more detail.

4.1. Limit WIP

Imagine, if you will, a crowded highway at rush hour in a major city. Traffic is bumper to bumper, and nobody is getting anywhere quickly, as illustrated in *Figure 9. Fully Utilized Highway, What about Throughput?*

Figure 9. Fully Utilized Highway, What about Throughput? ©epSos.de Flickr

The highway, however, is being efficiently utilized; almost every square foot of this very expensive resource has a car on it. Given this highly efficient utilization, why are we not able to move faster? The reason is that **utilization and throughput are negatively correlated**, as illustrated in *Figure 10. The Effect of Utilization on Cycle Time.*

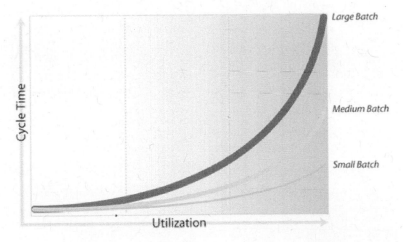

Figure 10. The Effect of Utilization on Cycle Time

That is, the **higher the shared utilization of a scarce resource, the slower we go**. Traffic systems, networking systems, and queuing theory in general predict this behavior. However, we in management have not thought to apply this same thinking to managing portfolios of projects until fairly recently. From queuing theory, Little's Law tells us,

Cycle Time = WIP/Average Completion Rate

So, to get projects moving faster, we can either reduce WIP (represented by active projects) or increase the rate at which we complete projects. Increasing the rate at which we complete projects is a fairly difficult endeavor. So, the most straightforward way to reduce project cycle time, and to increase project throughput is to reduce WIP by **reducing the number of active projects in the portfolio**.

The goal here is to **create a realigned portfolio that better balances stakeholder demand, and better matches it to team capacity**, as illustrated in *Figure 11. Rebalancing the Portfolio with Limited WIP.*

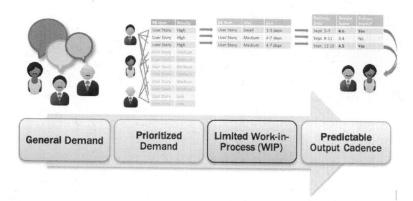

Figure 11. Rebalancing the Portfolio with Limited WIP

To apply this aspect of Lean Thinking, and to focus our teams on a much smaller WIP number of active projects, we can follow these steps:

· *Terminate zombie projects.* Zombie projects are ongoing, wandering projects that continually miss deadlines, lower morale, and simply cost too much. Terminate these zombie projects immediately. We need to purge the portfolio to reduce project inventory and redirect the effort of team members to more valuable initiatives. This is the best way to speed overall throughput, reduce waste, and maximize value.

· *Break large projects into small increments.* A minimum marketable feature (MMF) is a key component of marketable value. We can **group product features into increments of MMFs to deliver early value to end users.** We can also break up large projects into smaller projects organized around MMFs to reduce work in process and, in turn, reduce lead time.

· *Stop starting, start finishing.* Most organizations start more projects than they finish. To manage the project on-ramp, we can create and follow a lightweight, disciplined project prioritization process to decide which projects are started. Then, **we should start only those projects that can be properly resourced.** If a project starts to falter, terminate it before it becomes a zombie project.

· *Create a prioritized portfolio backlog.* Just as teams prioritize stories within a product backlog, we need to **prioritize projects based on business value to create a portfolio backlog**. Now, our teams can pull the highest priority project from this backlog. Teams can focus on a single project at a time and work closely with the business sponsor to deliver it. Only after a team completes the project and delivers the system into production can they pull the next highest priority project from the backlog.

4.2. Manage the Flow

A key concept of Lean Thinking is **continuous flow**. In Lean organizations, one-piece flow or continuous flow is implemented by making one part of a system facilitate end-to-end delivery to the customer correctly and completely, without interruptions, and with low cycle times.

Agile teams should practice this concept when they define, develop, integrate and deploy products by chunking them into **one feature or user story at a time**. The feature or more granular "user story" represents the "one piece" of business value that **needs to flow from the customer through development, testing and deployment back to the customer as quickly as possible without interruptions**. We can accomplish tracking and monitoring this for projects and products that are in progress by creating a visual management system similar to the one that was evolved by my colleague Bob Payne, which he named the Program Alignment Wall (PAW).

A sample PAW is illustrated in *Figure 12. Program Alignment Wall,* and was used to manage the work across a program of 21 teams, 4 Agile and 17 waterfall teams.

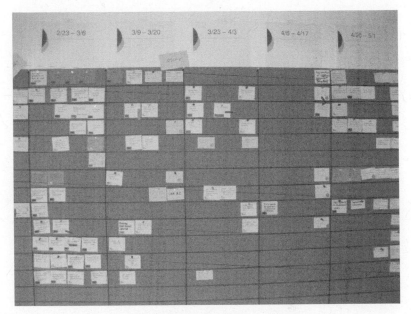

Figure 12. Program Alignment Wall

The PAW tracks work by laying it out in a two-dimensional format:

· Rows represent "swim lanes" of functionality;

· Columns represent Sprint or Iterations;

· Cards represent Epics (large chunks of work) and are laid out as an overall Release Plan; and

· Dot labels on cards capture inter-team and inter-project dependencies.

Note that **everything on the PAW is also simultaneously maintained in an Agile Lifecycle Management tool** like VersionOne, Rally, Agile Craft or Microsoft's Team Foundation Server (TFS).

To **manage the flow of features or user stories from creation to completion, and to avoid bottlenecks in product development using a PAW,** we need to ensure a *small batch size, a steady rate of arrival and service, and slack,* as described below.

· **Small Batch Size.** Small releases and iterative development provide two levels at which batch size can be controlled. We need to work with our customers to ensure that system functionality is being defined, created and released in small batches. At the release level, this means ensuring that feature batch size is kept small by breaking features into high-level user stories that take no longer than three weeks to implement, and that no release takes longer than 3-4 months, even for large projects.

At the Sprint or Iteration level it involves ensuring that **detailed user stories represent no more than three days of work**, and that iterations are kept to 1, 2 or 3 weeks in duration each.

As a user story is completed on a team's backlog, we simply **update the status of its parent Epic on the PAW to capture progress**.

· **Steady Rate of Arrival and Service**. Each row on the PAW is a queue. We monitor these queues to see that Epics both arrive and are serviced at a steady rate. As an Epic is in-flight, we make sure we record its cycle time from stage to stage, and its total cycle – the time it takes to move from inception to completion. We also monitor the **average cycle time** across all Epics, and thereby ensure things are moving smoothly.

· **Slack**. In order to remain fast and flexible, systems must maintain some degree of slack. The negative effects of systems without slack can be seen in overloaded networks, rush-hour highways, and most corporate IT departments. From queuing theory, we know that as more items enter a system, its ability to route them organically declines, leading to destructive interactions that slow everything down.

This tenet of queuing theory can be applied to resource allocation: If team members are split across multiple projects, their ability to deal with quick turnarounds, unexpected needs and complex problems will suffer. Dedication of core resources can help to alleviate these problems.

So, we avoid allocating team members above 80%, and always maintain 20% of slack time. At Google and Atlassian, this is called the **20% rule,** and is used to facilitate innovation. That is, team members are allowed up to **20% of their time to work on something of their choosing** that also adds business value.

4.3. Grow Small, Stable Teams

Harvard Business Review studies by Wheelwright and Clark and others have shown that our productivity is highest when we work on one or two things at a time, as illustrated in *Figure 13. The Effect of Multitasking on Productivity*.

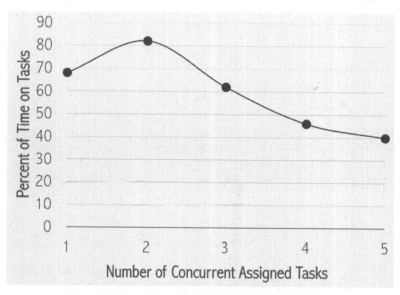

Figure 13. The Effect of Multitasking on Productivity

So, **Agile teams ought to focus on a single project at a time**, and by working closely with our business sponsors, should be able to finish it much more quickly and accurately than in traditional environments. When the team completes the project and delivers the system into production, it will then be available to start its next project.

Additionally, the Project Management Institute (PMI)'s Guide to the Project Management Body of Knowledge (PMBOK) tells us that to reach a high performance state, teams must go through the **Tuckman model of team formation: forming, storming, norming**

and performing. That is, it takes time and considerable effort to get a team into the performing state. So, why on earth do we break them up and try to recreate them again for the next project?

Instead of sinking costs into forming teams for projects only to break them up on completion, we need to **create stable teams as high performance units that focus on one product or project at a time**. So, we create integrated cross-functional teams with team members from different departments; including business analysts, designers, developers, testers, and a project manager (or ScrumMaster). We allocate these core team members at least 80 percent or more to the project. Now, to maximize project throughput, we only **start as many projects as there are available dedicated teams**.

We can then pull projects from a limited backlog of high-priority projects and allocate them as teams become available. *Figure 14. Bringing Prioritized Demand to Stable Agile Teams* illustrates this key concept.

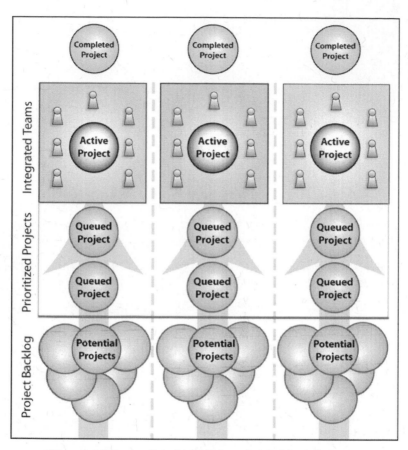

Figure 14. Bringing Prioritized Demand to Stable Agile Teams

The bottom line here is that our **stable teams form the basic unit of our allocation**.

4.4. Build a Network of Small Teams

"... for a large organization to work it must behave like a related group of small organizations." - E. F. Schumacher, **Small is Beautiful**

Once an Agile team is functioning well in its high-performance state, but reaches a size limit, say around nine people, **we form a new team and do not continue to expand the current team beyond its size limit.** To ensure that the new team is properly set up, a small seed group may break off from the original team to form its core. This core group, typically a manager, lead developer and business analyst, ensures that the team vision and culture are propagated intact to the new team. Importantly, **the core original team continues intact as a stable team.**

Following this approach avoids team bloat, and also ensures that teams retain their agile qualities. *Figure 15. Conquer-and-Divide Approach to Scaling Teams* illustrates this approach.

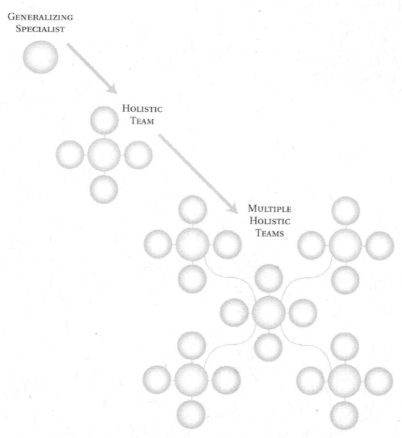

Figure 15. Conquer-and-Divide Approach to Scaling Teams

Now, how can we ensure that this team structure remains flexible enough to adapt to rapid change? An excellent way is employ a variation of the feature teams invented by Jeff De Luca for teams implementing the Feature Driven Development (FDD) Agile methodology.

In FDD, a chief programmer assumes responsibility for delivering specified features during an iteration. She then identifies the class owners – owners of specific code modules and pulls them together for the 1-3 week duration of the iteration to deliver the specified features. Besides the core group maintained for consistency and continuity, some members in the team may change from Sprint to Sprint depending on the functionality to be delivered, as illustrated in *Figure 16. Dynamic Team Membership.*

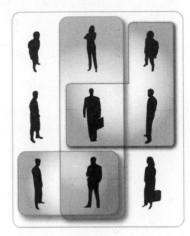

Figure 16. Dynamic Team Membership

To create connections between teams, noted Agile expert and author Johanna Rothman recommends a network instead of a hierarchy as the first step, as illustrated in *Figure 17. Network of Small Teams.*

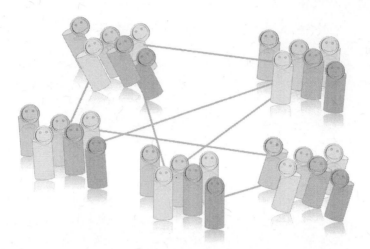

Figure 17. Network of Small Teams

As multiple teams are formed, **we want these networks to emerge organically from the teams themselves, and not be dictated top-down**. For instance, team members may connect around a shared discipline, as in a working group dedicated to improving test automation across teams. Or, they could connect as *kaizen* continuous improvement group to implement retrospective action items across teams.

4.5. Improve Continuously

At their essence, **all Agile methods incorporate W. Edwards Deming's Plan-Do-Check-Act continuous improvement cycle.** Learning is enabled by continuous feedback from the environment, and improvement is accomplished through incremental adaptation of strategies and rules. As we scale Agile methods, we can **Go to the Gemba** and institute **Kaizen for continuous improvement.**

Gemba is a Japanese term meaning "the real place." In business, it refers to the place where value is created; or where our Agile teams are located. In Lean Thinking, the idea of Gemba is that the problems are most visible, and hence the best improvement ideas will come from observing ongoing work on site and in person. The **Gemba Walk,** imagined in *Figure 18,* is an activity that takes management to those doing the actual value delivery **to look for waste and opportunities to practice kaizen, or practical improvement.**

Figure 18. Going to the Gemba

How important is it to connect management with the Gemba, or "real place" where work is done? To fully appreciate the answer, consider the alternative from the world of auto manufacturing. For years, executives in Detroit insulated themselves from the shop floor – their gemba. From the Seattle Times:

"For generations, the 14th floor of the General Motors Corp. head-quarters, with its thick carpets, mahogany walls and electronically controlled glass doors, has been the ultimate symbol of power at the world's largest company. Access was by invitation only.

Top executives were sealed off from the rest of the GM work force. Chauffeured into the basement garage, GM's leaders were whisked by private elevator to the 14th floor's executive row, where their meals were catered in a private dining room."

The hubris had an inevitable result - GM filed for bankruptcy after it was run into the ground.

Chrysler went through a similar fate in the 2008 automotive crisis. However, after its bankruptcy and bailout, Sergio Marchionne, pictured in *Figure 19*, the new CEO of Fiat and Chrysler took several bold steps to turn Chrysler around.

Figure 19. Sergio Marchionne, CEO of Fiat and Chrysler ©Italian Embassy Flickr

One of them was to forgo the remote chairman's office for the shop floor. The old office is now an empty "tourist trap."

In Marchionne's words, "It's empty now...because nothing happens there. I'm on the floor with all the engineers. **I can build a car with all the guys on the floor. That's all I care about.**"

Once these essential practices - **Limit WIP, Manage the Flow, Grow Small Stable Teams, Build a Network of Small Teams** and **Improve Continuously** are in place - **we can build on them to implement a scaling framework of choice.**

Complete framework choices include SAFe®, LeSS, DAD and Nexus. Next, we'll provide a brief overview of these frameworks as well a couple of techniques including the Scrum of Scrums meeting, and the Lean-Agile Program Management Office (PMO).

5. Overview of Scaling Techniques and Frameworks

Several scaling methods exist, ranging from almost ad-hoc to very prescriptive. The best method is one that is customizable to the organization, and that can be continuously improved through incremental adaptation.

As adoption of Agile methods in the industry continue to evolve, much energy has shifted to scaling techniques and frameworks. These range from the simple Scrum of Scrums technique, to the Scaled Agile Framework® (SAFe®), Large-Scale Scrum (LeSS) and Disciplined Agile Delivery (DAD), as shown in *Figure 20. Scaling Methods and Approaches.*

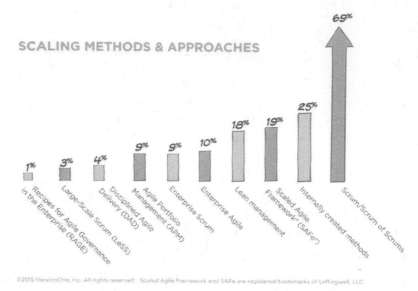

Figure 20. Scaling Methods and Approaches, VersionOne Survey 2014

5.1. The Scrum of Scrums Meeting

The most common technique to scale Scrum up to multiple teams is to replicate the Daily Scrum meeting across teams. After a team's Daily Scrum meeting ends, they designate one or two people to serve as "ambassadors." These ambassadors are dispatched to participate in a daily meeting with ambassadors from other teams, and this meeting is called the **Scrum of Scrums**.

The Scrum of Scrums proceeds otherwise as a normal daily meeting, with ambassadors reporting completions, next steps and impediments on behalf of the teams they represent.

Resolution of impediments is expected to focus on the challenges of coordination between the teams, which may include managing cross-team interfaces, responsibilities and so forth. A backlog dedicated to the Scrum of Scrums is generally used to track and manage these impediments and joint efforts across teams.

Learn more at Agile Alliance.[2]

---

[2]http://guide.agilealliance.org/guide/scrumofscrums.html

5.2. The Lean-Agile Program Management Office (PMO)

A more formal structure than the Scrum of Scrums is the **Lean-Agile Program Management Office**. While organizations will vary in size and complexity, the general structure of a Lean Agile PMO is shown in *Figure 21. The Lean-Agile PMO.*

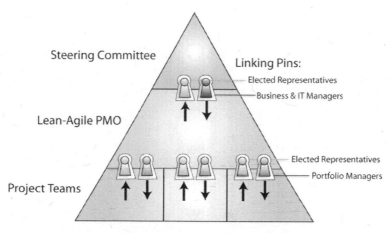

Figure 21. The Lean-Agile PMO

Linking-pin Representatives. The Lean-Agile PMO is connected via "linking-pin" representatives to the higher level steering committee and to Agile product and/or project teams. For instance, it includes at least two managers of Agile project teams. It also includes at least two executives, preferably one each from the delivery and business sides of the organization.

Elected Representatives. Key roles like the ScrumMaster for the Lean-Agile PMO, representatives from project teams, and representatives to the steering committee are elected from lower to higher levels: project teams elect representatives to the PMO, and the PMO elects its own representatives to the Steering Committee.

Agile Management. The Lean-Agile PMO is set up to use standard Agile practices. It has its own ScrumMaster who leads it in short iterations for delivery. The Lean-Agile PMO typically meets weekly, and its meetings follow the Scrum of Scrums format. It uses standard Scrum practices and artifacts, such as a prioritized long-term backlog that is created and updated in regular release planning meetings, a prioritized short-term backlog that is created and updated in regular sprint planning/review meetings, daily standup meetings, and regular tracking and monitoring.

Having a combination of linking-pin representatives who are assigned top-down and elected representatives who are elected bottom-up to straddle management levels helps ensure that the Lean-Agile PMO's hierarchy is not autocratic. Committing the Lean-Agile PMO itself to using Agile practices can help ensure that it stays self-organizing and adaptive to change.

Learn more at Cutter.com.[3]

---

[3]http://www.cutter.com/offers/leanagile.html

5.3. The Spotify Model

Spotify, the company behind the streaming music service, has become known for its innovative culture and innovations in the Agile space. Agile expert Henrik Kniberg has conveyed information about Spotify through several excellent whitepapers and videos. **Spotify's Agile** organizational and scaling model employs **Squads, Tribes, Chapters and Guilds,** as shown in *Figure 22. The Spotify Model.*

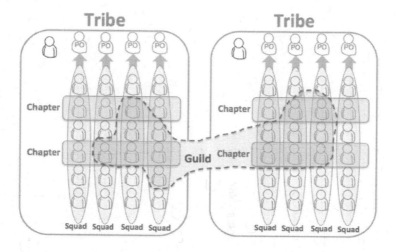

Figure 22. The Spotify Model

The basic unit, a **Squad,** is similar to a Scrum team. Each Squad has a long-term mission, ensuring it is a stable team. Squads spend 10% of their time on "hack days" to promote learning and innovation.

A **Tribe** is a collection of Squads that work in related areas – such as the music player, or backend infrastructure. Each Tribe has a Tribe lead who is responsible for providing the best possible habitat for the Squads within that Tribe. The Squads in a Tribe are all physically in the same office, normally right next to each other, and the lounge areas nearby promote collaboration between the Squads. Tribes are designed to be smaller than 100 people or so, based on the *Dunbar*

Number which says that most humans cannot maintain a social relationship with more than 100 people.

A **Chapter** is a small family of people within a given Tribe who have similar skills and work in the same general competency area. Each Chapter meets regularly to discuss their area of expertise and specific challenges - for example the Testing Chapter, the Web Developer Chapter or the Backend Chapter.

A **Guild** is a more organic and wide-reaching "community of interest," a group of people that want to share knowledge, tools, code and practices. Chapters are always local to a Tribe, while a Guild usually cuts across the whole organization. Some examples are: the Web Technology Guild, the Tester Guild, the Agile Coach Guilt, etc.

In essence, people are grouped into stable co-located Squads, where people with different skill sets collaborate and self-organize to deliver a great product. That's the **vertical dimension** in the matrix, and it is the primary one since that is how people are physically grouped and where they spend most of their time. The **horizontal dimension** is for **sharing knowledge, tools, and code**.

Learn more at: Scaling Agile @ Spotify with Tribes, Squads, Chapters & Guilds[4]

---

[4]https://dl.dropboxusercontent.com/u/1018963/Articles/SpotifyScaling.pdf

5.4. The Scaled Agile Framework® (SAFe®)

From Scaled Agile Framework®[5]

The Scaled Agile Framework® ("SAFe®") is a proven knowledge base for implementing Agile practices at scale. As illustrated in *Figure 23. Scaled Agile Framework Overview,* SAFe has three levels of scale: **Team, Program and Portfolio.**

Each of these scales the essential Agile elements of **Value** (requirements and backlogs), **Teams** (from development team through portfolio) and **Timebox** (iteration, Program Increment, budget cycle).

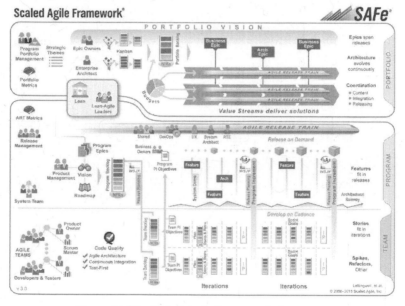

Figure 23. The Scaled Agile Framework Overview

SAFe® has been successfully applied in programs of only 50-100 people, and in enterprises employing thousands of software

---

[5]http://www.scaledagileframework.com/about

developers.

Learn more at ScaledAgileFramework.com.[6]

---

[6]http://scaledagileframework.com

5.5 Large Scale Scrum (LeSS)

Large-Scale Scrum (LeSS) provides two different large scale Scrum frameworks. Most of the scaling elements of LeSS are focused on directing the attention of all of the teams toward the whole product instead of "my part." Global and "end-to-end" focus are perhaps the dominant problems to solve in scaling.

The two frameworks – which are basically single-team Scrum scaled up – are:

· LeSS: Up to eight teams (of eight people each);

· LeSS Huge: Up to a few thousand people on one product.

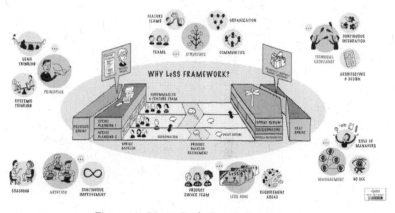

Figure 24. Large-Scale Scrum Overview

LeSS is a scaled up version of one-team Scrum, and it maintains many of the practices and ideas of one-team Scrum. In LeSS, you will find:

· a single Product Backlog (because it's for a product, not a team);

· one Definition of Done for all teams;

· one Potentially Shippable Product Increment (PSPI) at the end of each Sprint;

· one (overall) Product Owner;

· many complete, cross-functional teams (with no specialist teams);

· and one Sprint.

In LeSS, all Teams are in a common Sprint to deliver a common PSPI.

Learn more at LeSS.works.[7]

---

[7]http://less.works

5.6. Disciplined Agile Delivery (DAD)

The Disciplined Agile Delivery (DAD) process decision framework is a people-first, learning-oriented hybrid Agile approach to IT solution delivery, as illustrated in *Figure 25. Disciplined Agile Delivery Overview (Example)*. DAD has a risk-value delivery lifecycle, is goal-driven, is enterprise aware, and is scalable.

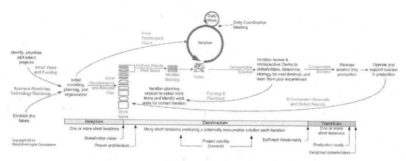

Figure 25. Disciplined Agile Delivery Overview (Example)

DAD extends the construction-focused lifecycle of Scrum to address the full, end-to-end delivery lifecycle from project initiation all the way to delivering the solution to its end users. It also supports lean and continuous delivery versions of the lifecycle: unlike other Agile methods, DAD doesn't prescribe a single lifecycle because it recognizes that one process size does not fit all.

DAD teams will adopt a lifecycle that is most appropriate for their situation and then tailor it.

Learn more at DisciplinedAgileDelivery.com.[8]

---

[8]http://www.disciplinedagiledelivery.com/introduction-todad

5.7. Scaled Professional Scrum - Nexus™

From Scrum.org.[9]

Nexus is the exoskeleton of scaled Scrum. It drives to the heart of the scaling issue - continually identifying and removing dependencies created by increased complexity. It builds on the existing Scrum framework and values.

As illustrated in *Figure 26. Nexus™ Overview,* the result is an effective development group of up to 100 people using best industry practices. For larger initiatives, creating product families or inter-operating functional units, we create Nexus +, a unification of more than one Nexus.

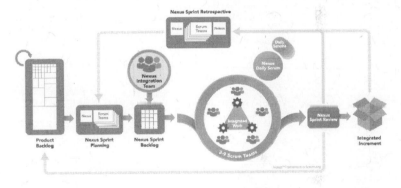

Figure 26. Nexus™ Overview

Learn more at Scrum.org.[10]

---

[9]https://www.scrum.org/Resources/What-is-Scaled-Scrum
[10]https://www.scrum.org/Resources/What-is-Scaled-Scrum

References

Image Attribution:

Driving Cars in a Traffic Jam (c) epSos .de on Flickr;[11] Creative Commons Attribution 2.0 Generic.[12]

Event in honor of Italian President Giorgio Napolitano a Villa Firenze (c) Italian Embassy on Flickr;[13] Creative Commons Attribution-NoDerivs 2.0 Generic.[14]

---

[11]https://flic.kr/p/9w8eWL
[12]https://creativecommons.org/licenses/by/2.0/
[13]https://flic.kr/p/dWvaKs
[14]https://creativecommons.org/licenses/by-nd/2.0/

About

Scaling Agile: A Lean JumpStart is the first book in the **LitheSpeed Agile Executive Series.**

Sanjiv Augustine, *CSM, CSP, CST, DSDM Leader, PMI ACP*

Sanjiv Augustine is an entrepreneur, industry-leading Agile and Lean expert, author, speaker, management consultant and trainer. With 25 years in the industry, Sanjiv has served as a trusted advisor over the past 15 years to executives and management at leading firms including: Capital One, The Capital Group, CNBC, Comcast, Freddie Mac, Fannie Mae, General Dynamics, HCA Healthcare, The Motley Fool, National Geographic, Nationwide Insurance, Walmart and Samsung.

He is the author of the book **Managing Agile Projects**[15] (Prentice Hall 2005) and several publications including Transitioning to Agile Project Management and The Lean Agile PMO: Using Lean Thinking to Accelerate Agile Project Delivery.

---

[15]http://www.amazon.com/Managing-Agile-Projects-Sanjiv-Augustine/dp/0131240714

He is the Chair of the **Agile Alliance's Agile Executive Forum**[16] and the founder and moderator of the Lean Startup in the Enterprise Meetup.[17] Sanjiv was also a founder and advisory board member of the **Agile Leadership Network (ALN)**[18], and a founder member of the Project Management Institute's Agile Community of Practice.

For more information, see LitheSpeed.com.[19]

---

[16]http://execforum.agilealliance.org/
[17]http://www.meetup.com/Lean-Startup-in-the-Enterprise
[18]http://www.agileleadershipnetwork.org/
[19]http://www.lithespeed.com

About TechWell

From our founding as Software Quality Engineering (SQE) to now as TechWell Corporation, the company's focus has remained the same—helping software developers, testers, and managers improve development and delivery practices.

Learn — Through respected software conferences, expert-led training classes, and in-depth online resources, TechWell offers multiple ways to learn about methods, technologies, and tools software professionals need to design, develop, test, and deliver great software.

Connect — TechWell offers numerous opportunities to connect with software industry experts, your peers, and leading solution providers at live events and to participate on community websites. We are always working on new ways to get people talking and working together.

Contribute — TechWell conferences, community websites, and publications provide multiple ways for experienced practitioners, industry consultants, and solution providers to contribute their expertise and practical advice about broad software topic areas.

Visit TechWell.com[20] for more.

---

[20]www.techwell.com